3/12

W9-BNQ-407

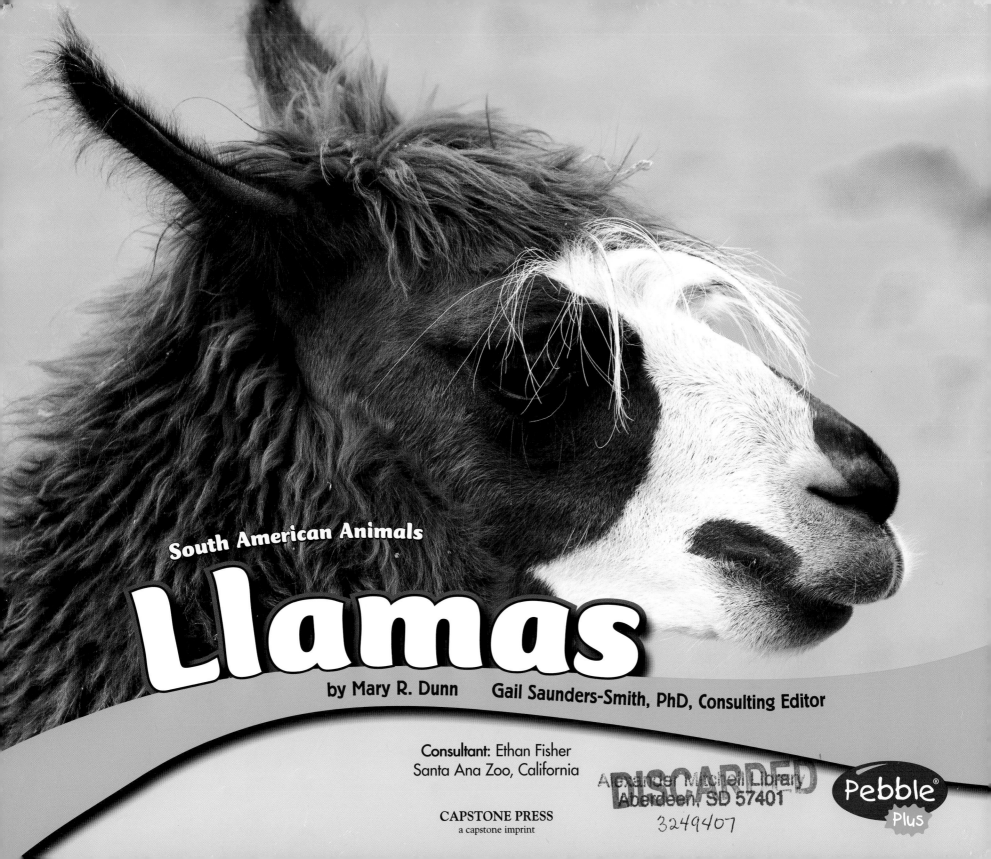

South American Animals

Llamas

by Mary R. Dunn   Gail Saunders-Smith, PhD, Consulting Editor

Consultant: Ethan Fisher
Santa Ana Zoo, California

DISCARDED
Alexander Mitchell Library
Aberdeen, SD 57401
3249407

Pebble
Plus

CAPSTONE PRESS
a capstone imprint

Pebble Plus is published by Capstone Press,
1710 Roe Crest Drive, North Mankato, Minnesota 56003.
www.capstonepub.com

Copyright © 2012 by Capstone Press, a Capstone imprint. All rights reserved.
No part of this publication may be reproduced in whole or in part, or stored in a retrieval system, or transmitted in any
form or by any means, electronic, mechanical, photocopying, recording, or otherwise, without written permission of the
publisher. For information regarding permission, write to Capstone Press,
1710 Roe Crest Drive, North Mankato, Minnesota 56003.

Books published by Capstone Press are manufactured with paper
containing at least 10 percent post-consumer waste.

Library of Congress Cataloging-in-Publication Data
Dunn, Mary R.
  Llamas / by Mary R. Dunn.
      p. cm.—(Pebble plus. South American animals)
  Includes bibliographical references and index.
  Summary: "Simple text and photographs present llamas, how they look, where they live, and what they do"—Provided
by publisher.
  ISBN 978-1-4296-7588-8 (library binding)
  1. Llamas—Juvenile literature. I. Title. II. Series.
QL737.U54D86 2012
636.2'966—dc23   2011027036

Editorial Credits
Katy Kudela, editor; Lori Bye, designer; Kathy McColley, production specialist

Photo Credits
Alamy/Mireille Vautier, 7
Corbis/Michael Freeman, 11
Dreamstime/Photoblueice, 13; Uwe Bumann, 1; Wasabikissx3jp, 19
iStockphoto/Marco Maccarini, 17
newscom/Danita Delimont Photography/Peter Langer, 5, 21
Shutterstock/Justin Black, 9; Leagam, cover
Super Stock Inc./Belinda Images, 15

Note to Parents and Teachers

The South American Animals series supports national science standards related to life science.
This book describes and illustrates llamas. The images support early readers in understanding
the text. The repetition of words and phrases helps early readers learn new words. This book
also introduces early readers to subject-specific vocabulary words, which are defined in the
Glossary section. Early readers may need assistance to read some words and to use the Table of
Contents, Glossary, Read More, Internet Sites, and Index sections of the book.

Printed in the United States of America in North Mankato, Minnesota.
102011   006405CGS12

Table of Contents

Mountain Mammals

Llamas scamper over rocky mountains in South America. These woolly mammals graze high in the mountains to stay cool in the summer.

World Map

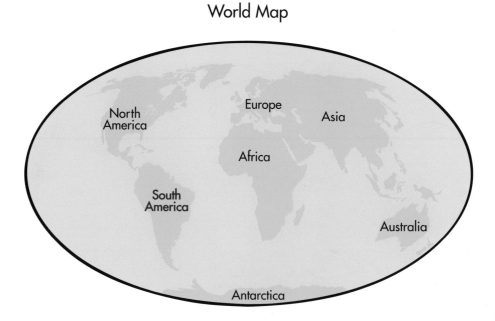

North America

Europe

Asia

Africa

South America

Australia

Antarctica

Llamas are tame animals.

They are raised in herds that live

mostly in the Andes Mountains.

People use llamas to carry

heavy loads.

South America Map

 where llamas live

Up Close!

Llamas are a type of camel.

They have shaggy fur,

long necks, and small heads.

Llamas grow up to 6 feet

(1.8 meters) tall.

Llamas are good pack animals.
Pads on their toes grip rocky
ground. Their strong legs carry
loads far. Llamas can walk up
to 18 miles (29 kilometers) a day.

Finding Food

Llamas are not picky eaters. They chomp on salty grasses and plants. They get most of the water they need from the plants they eat.

Growing Up

Female llamas have one baby a year. Crias are born furry, with their eyes open. These babies drink their mothers' milk for about four months.

Crias walk within an hour after birth. But these babies don't stray. They stay close to their mothers for about a year. Llamas live up to 20 years.

Staying Safe

In a llama herd, one male
cares for the group.
He watches for predators.
He makes loud noises
if danger is near.

Llamas can run up to 30 miles

(48 kilometers) per hour.

But hungry mountain lions

run just as fast. Llamas bite,

kick, or spit to stay safe.

Glossary

cria—a baby llama

graze—to feed on growing grass or herbs

herd—a large group of animals that lives or moves together

mammal—a warm-blooded animal that breathes air; mammals have hair or fur; female mammals feed milk to their young

pack animal—an animal used for carrying loads

pad—the soft part on the bottom of the feet of llamas and many other animals

predator—an animal that hunts other animals for food

scamper—to run lightly and quickly

stray—to wander away or get lost

tame—trained to live with or be useful to people

Read More

Hudak, Heather C. *Llamas*. Farm Animals. New York: Weigl Pub., 2007.

Marsico, Katie. *Farm Animals: Llamas*. 21st Century Junior Library. Ann Arbor, Mich.: Cherry Lake Pub., 2011.

Stockland, Patricia M. *In the Llama Yard*. Barnyard Buddies. Edina, Minn.: Magic Wagon, 2010.

Internet Sites

FactHound offers a safe, fun way to find Internet sites related to this book. All of the sites on FactHound have been researched by our staff.

Here's all you do:

Visit *www.facthound.com*

Type in this code: 9781429675888

Check out projects, games and lots more at **www.capstonekids.com**

Index

Word Count: 225

Grade: 1

Early-Intervention Level: 18